MOSES and the FLIGHT from EGYPT

MOSES and the FLIGHT from EGYPT

illustrated by Leon Baxter
adapted by Diana Craig

Silver Burdett Company

Moses and his family trudged across the desert for days. Now they were nearly there. That night, as they slept by a camp fire, God's plan tumbled through Moses' dreams. "Return to Egypt . . . trick the Pharaoh . . . free your people, the Israelite slaves . . ."

Moses woke with a start and remembered the great task God had given him. He had to persuade the Pharaoh, king of Egypt, to give the Israelites three days off work to hold a festival in the desert to pray to God. Three days would give them just the chance they needed to escape from Egypt . . .

"Come on, it's nearly dawn," he said, shaking his sleeping wife and children and his brother Aaron. "Let's get going."

As they drew near the Pharaoh's palace, they saw the slaves in the blistering sun. They were mixing straw and clay to make bricks. An exhausted slave dropped to the ground.

"Back to work, oaf!" bellowed the slave driver, cracking his whip on the slave's back. "There's to be no rest for you lazy slaves – Pharaoh's orders!" It was worse than Moses had feared.

When Moses and Aaron reached the palace, they felt very nervous, for they knew they couldn't trust the Pharaoh. But God had promised to look after them so, plucking up their courage, they entered the royal throne room.

The Pharaoh was munching a honey-soaked cake as they came in.

"Er . . . um . . . your H-Highness," stammered Moses.

"Get on with it!" snapped the Pharaoh, "I'm a busy man."

"Royal Pharaoh," gulped Aaron, "God says you must let the Israelites hold a festival in the desert . . . or else!"

"Or else *what*?" roared the Pharaoh? "What God dares to threaten me, the mighty Pharaoh? There'll be no festivals for those lazy bones . . . I'll show them who's boss!" He called to his chief slave driver. "From now on, those idle slaves must find their own straw to make bricks with. *And I still want five hundred bricks a day from each slave, or they'll get five hundred extra lashes!*"

The Israelites were in despair. The extra work would kill them. It was all Moses' fault. Why had he interfered?

Moses felt miserable. "I've only made things worse and now everybody hates me," he grumbled to God.

"Oh, Moses," replied God gently, "don't give up so soon. The Pharaoh thinks he is mightier than I am, but I'll teach him a few lessons he will never forget. This is only the start of his troubles, but he'll give in in the end . . . you'll see."

Then Moses felt very foolish for not trusting God.

Next morning, Moses and Aaron went down to the river, where the Pharaoh was about to have his daily wash.

"Good morning, Pharaoh," said Moses. "God has decided to give you one more chance to obey him."

"Stop pestering me," came the scornful reply. "Your silly threats don't bother me!" At once, Aaron threw his staff to the ground, where it turned into a snake. The Pharaoh was terrified, but he called his royal magicians, and they too turned their staffs into snakes.

"You see," said the Pharaoh, "my magicians are just as powerful as your God." And he splashed into the water.

Aaron touched the cool, dark water with his staff, just as God had instructed. As he did so, the water changed to a warm, sticky red. It was blood! And as if that wasn't enough, the fish began to die. The smell was disgusting.

"That's nothing," said the Pharaoh, holding his nose. He called his magicians, who mumbled some spells. They turned the rest of the water in Egypt into blood, even the water in the pans of vegetables cooking for dinner.

"See?" said the Pharaoh, smugly.

Moses was furious that the Pharaoh's stupid magicians had made a fool of him. But God was not worried, and a week later he sent Moses and Aaron back to the Pharaoh.

"Well?" demanded Moses when he met the Pharaoh again. "Now will you let the Israelites have their festival?"

"Why should I?" jeered the Pharaoh. "I'm not afraid of your God. My magicians can do anything he can!"

"Then don't say we didn't warn you," said Moses sternly. And with that, Aaron held his staff out across the rivers and ponds, just as God had told him to. Suddenly, the air was filled with croaking noises as thousands of frogs leaped from the water. They were all over the place!

Not to be outdone, the Pharaoh sent for his magicians. A few spells later, there were even more frogs hopping about!

But the magicians could not get rid of the frogs. When a particularly large frog wriggled down his clothes, the Pharaoh lost his temper. "All right!" he yelled at Moses. "Get rid of the frogs, and the Israelites can have their festival. But there'll be trouble if they come back late!"

"The frogs will be gone by tomorrow," said Moses, calmly. "Then you will know that God is the most powerful."

But the next day, when all the frogs had gone, the Pharaoh broke his promise to Moses.

Angrily, Aaron hit the ground with his staff. A huge cloud of hungry gnats flew out of the dust. They fell on the Egyptians and bit them until they scratched and bled.

"Now," said Moses, "will you see sense and do as you're told?" But the Pharaoh paid no attention. He wouldn't even listen to his magicians when they warned him that they could no longer compete with God.

And so it went on. After the gnats, God sent swarms of flies. The Egyptians could not keep them out of their food and drink. They were driven mad as the flies tickled their noses and crawled into their ears. Once again, the Pharaoh broke his promise to Moses when the flies had gone.

A few days later, the Egyptians woke up to find that all their cows, goats, sheep and camels had died. The farmers were terrified and begged the Pharaoh to change his mind. "The Israelites are nothing but trouble. Their God has killed all our animals, and left theirs alone. Please, please let them go," they pleaded.

But the Pharaoh still refused to let the Israelites go.

Moses wondered how much longer the Pharaoh would go on being so stubborn. Didn't he know he couldn't win?

God told Moses to throw some ashes into the air. As it fell on the Egyptians, they broke out into ugly, red boils. Even the magicians were covered in them, and they were so embarrassed that they hid in their rooms. Still the Pharaoh said no.

Moses tried to reason with him. "God could kill you in an instant. He only keeps you alive so you will be forced to admit how mighty he is. Can't you see that nobody can fight God?" But the Pharaoh would not listen.

That day, God told Moses to send the worst storm Egypt had ever seen. Thunder and lightning raged in the sky, while hailstones as big as eggs clattered on the roofs and flattened the crops in the fields.

It made no difference to the Pharaoh. "I won't let God get the better of me! Soon he'll give up, and I'll have won. I'll be more powerful than God," he gloated to himself.

Then Moses reached out and the sky was filled with clouds of locusts. They gobbled up what was left of the crops and stripped the leaves off the trees. Egypt was like a desert.

The Egyptians began to panic. "If the Pharaoh won't see sense, there'll be nothing left of Egypt!" they cried.

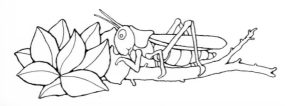

The next time God punished the Pharaoh, the terrified Egyptians thought it was the end of the world. Egypt was plunged into a terrible blackness that was blacker than night. For three days and nights not a bird sang, and not a breath of wind stirred, in the awful black silence.

But even with his country in ruins, the Pharaoh would not admit defeat.

By now, Moses had had enough of the Pharaoh's lying and stubborness. He was relieved when God told him that he would give the Pharaoh the last and worst punishment of all.

"Fourteen days from now, I will go through Egypt at midnight," God told Moses. "The Israelites must paint a mark in lamb's blood on their doors. When I see this sign I will pass by. But I will visit every other house. When I leave, the oldest child in every Egyptian family will be dead."

It all happened just as God promised. There was death in every house and the Egyptians wept and wailed and tore their hair out. Even the Pharaoh lost his son.

That same night, the Pharaoh ran, sobbing, to Moses. "Go, take your people away," he begged on bended knees, "or God will kill us all!"

The Israelites hardly dared believe the Pharaoh. Quickly, they grabbed everything they could carry for the long trip.

Thousands of excited voices babbled away as the slaves lined up with their animals. Then they set off, wading through the river marshes until they reached the desert. God showed them the way with a towering pillar of cloud. At night, he lit their path with a pillar of burning fire.

At last, as the sun set, they stopped on the shore of a great sea. They had just pitched their tents for the night, when they heard a low rumbling, far away. It got louder and louder until, with horror, they realized it was the sound of galloping horses. The Pharaoh had broken his word! There he was, with six hundred war chariots filled with shouting soldiers, chasing after them.

The Egyptians camped nearby, and the Israelites knew they were trapped. With the Pharaoh on one side, and the sea on the other, they didn't stand a chance. At first light the next day, the Egyptians would attack and destroy them all.

The Israelites panicked. "You fool!" they shouted at Moses. "If only you'd left us in Egypt, we'd be safe now!"

"Keep calm!" shouted Moses above the row. "God will save us!" But the Israelites were too scared to listen. Nobody slept a wink that night.

Moses trusted God, but he had no idea how he would get them out of this! Early next morning, God told him.

"March on," was all God said.

Moses was amazed at his words. "How can we?" he asked. "We're trapped by the water."

But God calmly repeated his words. "March on. Point your staff at the water, and march on."

As Moses pointed his staff, a howling wind blew up. It almost knocked him over! It blew on the sea with all its might until it had pushed the waters apart. Between two great walls of water, lay a safe path across the sea. The Israelites were astonished. Laughing and jumping with joy, they scrambled all the way to the shore on the other side.

The Pharaoh shouted to his army to follow him down the path. But God was waiting for them. The chariot wheels stuck in the mud and the horses slithered off their feet. Then, with a roar, the waters closed over the Pharaoh and his army. Every Egyptian was swallowed up in the rush of waves.

When the Israelites saw what God had done, they were ashamed that they had ever doubted him. They begged Moses for forgiveness. God had taught the Pharaoh his final lesson, and the Israelites were free at last.

This story has been told in many different ways for more than three thousand years. It was first written down in a language called Hebrew. Since then, it has been retold in almost every language used in the world today.

You can find the story of Moses in the Bible. This part of his life is in the Book of Exodus, Chapters 5 to 15.

There is a companion to this book called "The Young Moses". It tells the story of Moses' birth and how, when he grew up, God sent him to rescue the Israelites from Egypt.

Editor: John Morton
Publishing Manager: Belinda Hollyer
Production: Susan Mead
Teacher Consultant: Pauline Morton
Old Testament Consultant: The Rev'd. A. K. Jenkins

© Macdonald & Co (Publishers) Ltd 1984

Adapted and published
in the United States by
Silver Burdett Company
Morristown, N.J.

1984 printing

ISBN 0-382-06796-7

Library of Congress
Catalog Card No. 84-50448

1 2 3 4 5 6 7 8 9 10—JDL—90 89 88 87 86 85 84